Cambridge **Discovery Education**™

▶ **INTERACTIVE READERS**

Series editor: Bob Hastings

DOWN TO EARTH

B1+

Caroline Shackleton and Nathan Paul Turner

CAMBRIDGE UNIVERSITY PRESS
Cambridge, New York, Melbourne, Madrid, Cape Town,
Singapore, São Paulo, Delhi, Mexico City

Cambridge University Press
32 Avenue of the Americas, New York, NY 10013-2473, USA

www.cambridge.org
Information on this title: www.cambridge.org/9781107661172

First published 2014
Reprinted 2014

Printed in Hong Kong, China, by Golden Cup Printing Company Limited

A catalog record for this publication is available from the British Library.

Library of Congress Cataloging-in-Publication Data

Shackleton, Caroline.
 Down to earth / Caroline Shackleton and Nathan Paul Turner.
    pages cm. -- (Cambridge discovery interactive readers)
 ISBN 978-1-107-66117-2 (pbk. : alk. paper)
 1. Transportation--Juvenile literature. 2. English language--Textbooks for foreign speakers.
 3. Readers (Elementary) I. Title.

HE152.S44 2013
388--dc23

                        2013024752

ISBN 978-1-107-66117-2

Additional resources for this publication at www.cambridge.org

Layout services, art direction, book design, and photo research: Q2ABillSMITH GROUP
Editorial services: Hyphen S.A.
Audio production: CityVox, New York
Video production: Q2ABillSMITH GROUP

Contents

Before You Read:
Get Ready!

The way people move on land and sea has changed over time as technology has changed. In this book you'll read about getting around on everything from the horse to the hovercraft!

Words to Know

Read the paragraph. Then use the correct form of the highlighted words to complete the definitions below.

Until the 1960s people and goods were carried by steam-powered trains. But today, trains and most other vehicles are powered by gasoline, and most commuters go from their homes to their jobs by car. These changes have led to two serious problems: pollution from gas-powered engines and congestion caused by the huge amount of traffic traveling to and from our cities every day.

1 _____ : moved by using the energy that comes from heating water

2 _____ : things that are bought and sold

3 _____ : something used to transport people or things

4 _____ : what we use to power our cars; also called "petrol" or just "gas"

5 _____ : the result of having too much traffic

Look at the pictures. Then use the correct words to complete the sentences below.

bicycle lane

carriage

commuters

ferry

transportation

wagon

1 A _____ is a boat or ship for taking passengers and often vehicles across water, especially as a regular service.

2 _____ are people who travel regularly between work and home, often by train, bus, or car.

3 _____ is any vehicle used for getting from one place to another.

4 A _____ is the part of a street where only people on bicycles can travel.

5 A _____ is a vehicle with four wheels, often pulled by animals and usually used to transport goods.

6 A _____ is the part of a vehicle that passengers ride in.

? PREDICT
Before you read, think of places that are famous for a particular type of transportation.

A raft is a boat made of logs.

CHAPTER 1

A Short History of Transportation

HOW WE TRAVEL SAYS A LOT ABOUT WHO WE ARE.

We usually don't think much about the cars, buses, and trains that take us from our homes to the places where we work, study, and enjoy ourselves. And yet, without these forms of transportation, our lives would be very different. Transportation technology is constantly **developing**, bringing changes to the cities we live in and the way we move around them.

The first humans walked and ran everywhere, often over great distances. A few traditional peoples, such as the San in South Africa, still live this way today.

The first **vehicles** were probably small rafts that carried people along rivers and across seas. Some scientists believe rafts were used to sail from Asia to Australia as early as 70,000 years ago.

Scientists think that people began to domesticate[1] horses 4,000 to 6,000 years ago. People in Kazakhstan captured[2] groups of wild horses. They wanted them for meat and milk, but they also used them for riding and carrying things.

Other animals, such as the North African camel, were domesticated about 3,500 years ago. Animals such as these allowed people to move farther and carry more. This helped in the development of trade between societies.

And then came the wheel. Although the wheel is quite a recent invention, we don't know exactly where or when people first used it. But we know that the huge stone blocks that were used to make Stonehenge in England as early as 3100 BCE needed something like wheels to move them. Maybe they used wooden rollers made from logs as a type of wheel.

[1] **domesticate:** bring wild animals under human control
[2] **capture:** catch and keep someone or something

An ancient cart wheel

A chariot

The first proper wheel we know of was used in Mesopotamia (modern-day Iraq) about 3500 BCE, although some scientists think wheels may be much older. By 1000 BCE the wheel was common across Europe and the Middle East.

Over time, wheel technology improved and wheels became lighter, faster, and more stable.[3] By 500 BCE, metal-covered wheels and vehicles pulled by horses and other animals were common. There were fast chariots to fight in wars, slow carts to carry food and other goods, and comfortable carriages for rich people to get around in. And all thanks to the wheel!

Of course, vehicles need roads to run on. Early roads were simple dirt tracks,[4] but many societies, such as the Indians, the Chinese, and the Romans, soon built **networks** of good, straight roads to connect their cities.

[3] **stable:** not likely to move or change
[4] **track:** a narrow path or road

After the Roman Empire, there were great improvements in boat building. Ships and boats sailed faster and farther across seas, up and down rivers, and along canals.

In the 18th century, British canals were a key part of the Industrial Revolution.[5] Then, in 1825, George Stephenson ran the first steam-powered train. The new trains could carry goods faster and farther than animal transportation, making travel much easier.

In the 19th century, some cities started services to help people travel to work. The first horse-powered bus began in France in 1826, carrying 14 passengers. By the end of the century, buses were used internationally and were powered by gasoline.

In 1863, the first underground train **system** opened in London, and in 1873, San Francisco started its now famous streetcar service. A new age – the age of the **commuter** – had begun.

[5] **Industrial Revolution:** a time when there were big changes and growth in the way we make things

CHAPTER 2

Green to Go

IF THERE WAS ONE VEHICLE THAT CHANGED THE WAY WE LIVED MORE THAN ANY OTHER IN THE 20TH CENTURY, IT WAS THE AUTOMOBILE.

The first commercial gasoline-powered automobile was produced in 1885 by Karl Benz. At first, automobiles were expensive luxuries, but new factory methods and the introduction of credit loans soon made them easier to get and cheaper to own. In the USA, 56 percent of families owned a car as early as 1927.

Cars were often sold using the ideas of freedom[6] and speed. But as more and more people took to the roads, the disadvantages of car travel became clear. The large number of cars on the roads soon led to pollution and congestion. By the end of the 20th century, driving for many people around the world had become a nightmare[7] of traffic jams, rising **fuel** costs, and less healthy air to breathe.

[6] **freedom:** a way to live without being controlled by anyone else
[7] **nightmare:** a bad dream, something unpleasant

Guangzhou, China's third-largest city, is taking the problem of pollution very seriously. The city, which is one of the fastest-growing areas in China, had already banned[8] motorbikes in 2007. In 2012, the city government passed a new law that aims to cut the number of new cars on its streets by half. At the same time, Guangzhou is increasing its bus services to encourage people to use "greener" – more environmentally friendly – transportation.

In a move to reduce gasoline use, some cities are providing transportation programs that do not use traditional buses. Instead, they have chosen to encourage green transportation. Vehicles such as boats, trains, and bikes make less pollution and, most importantly, they don't fill up city streets or cause traffic jams.

[8]**ban:** not allow somebody to do something

One way to cut down on highly polluting road transportation is to return to the past. Ferry boats have long been used around the world in cities built near water.

In London, for example, water taxis on the River Thames were a common sight in Elizabethan times. Nowadays, London Transport still runs regular river buses every 20 minutes through the center of the city for both tourists and commuters.

New York City is also encouraging commuters to use its ferry services. The East River Ferry connects Manhattan with Queens, Brooklyn, and Governor's Island. Three boats run every 20 minutes and allow people to move easily around the city for just a few dollars. For an extra dollar, cyclists can also take their bikes on board and enjoy the beautiful views along the river.

Video Quest

Commuting in Tokyo

Watch this video about transportation in Tokyo. How many taxis are there? How many people travel by train and how many by plane?

Of course, cycling is probably the greenest form of transportation we have. Cycling is cheap, fast, and clean. It even helps keep you fit.

However, cycling is not always easy. It can be dangerous to share roads with cars, trucks, and buses. To make cycling safer and easier, many of the world's biggest cities have built separate bicycle lanes.

Another way some cities are trying to encourage cycling is by creating cycle sharing systems. In 2007, Paris started the Vélib system. Users buy a 1-day or 7-day ticket, which allows them to rent any of the Vélib's 20,000 bicycles from a network of 1,800 stations throughout the city, 24 hours a day. Afterward, the renter simply locks the bike back into a station, any station. The first 30 minutes of each journey are completely free.

CHAPTER 3

Muscle Power

TRAVELING UNDER YOUR
OWN STEAM MAY BE THE
BEST WAY TO GO!

When we think of traveling nowadays, we think about buses, trains, and cars. However, in many parts of the world, it is simply not possible to use **motor** vehicles. They may be too expensive to run, make too much pollution, or need a lot of work to keep them running well. Some areas have difficult terrain[9] where gasoline-powered vehicles cannot travel. In these cases, **muscle** power may be the answer!

Historically, all land vehicles were muscle powered. Most used animals, but some used people! In ancient societies such as Rome, Egypt, and China, important people rode through city streets carried on a litter, a special type of bed or chair. The litter was normally carried by two or four people. Many kings and queens throughout history used litters, including the Egyptian queen Cleopatra.

[9]**terrain:** a type of land, for example, hilly, mountainous, rocky, flat

In Venice, a city built on 118 small islands, all the taxis are boats! Venice has no roads, but hundreds of canals and waterways. You can even take a boat to get to the airport!

While you can take a motorboat, many people prefer to take the original Venetian taxi, the famous *gondola*. Gondolas are long, narrow boats. Traditionally, they had a small cabin to protect passengers from the weather. Nowadays, gondolas have become a tourist attraction and are completely open to give the best possible views.

A *gondolier* stands at the back of the boat, expertly pushing it through the water using a long oar. Gondoliers must pass a test to get their license, and they must know everything about the city's canals. Visitors and residents agree that a gondola ride is an amazing way to see this beautiful city.

?
UNDERSTAND
Why do people use gondolas in Venice?

Gondoliers push the gondolas with a long oar.

A rickshaw in the past

A rickshaw in the present

Another traditional taxi service that uses muscle power instead of engines is the rickshaw. Historians think that rickshaws were first used in Japan in the mid-19th century. Traditionally, they were small carriages for one or two people. However, instead of being pulled by an animal, they were pulled by the taxi driver!

Pulling rickshaws was very hard work for the drivers. Today, traditional rickshaws have been replaced with cycle rickshaws. Instead of running in front of the carriage to pull the passengers along, the driver now sits at the front of the cabin and cycles.

These cyclo-taxis are very popular in countries like Vietnam, India, and Thailand. Because they don't use gasoline, they are very green. Cities around the world, such as London and New York, have recently begun using them as well.

Thailand is also famous for another unusual type of transportation: elephants! In the past it was difficult to get through Thailand's thick jungles, so many people used to travel on elephants. Although motor transportation is often used today, elephants are still an important way to travel. In fact, in areas with thick forest or wide rivers, elephants are still the best form of transportation, as they can go places where even the toughest[10] vehicles cannot!

Unfortunately, elephants have been under threat[11] in recent years from illegal hunting, and many elephant tour companies do not look after their animals well. Now, some people have started green tourist projects that keep elephants safe and give them good living conditions. If you visit Thailand and want to ride an elephant, please make sure you choose one of these.

....

[10]**tough:** able to stay strong in difficult conditions

[11]**under threat:** in danger

Video Quest

Bedouin Travel

Watch this video about the Bedouins in the Sinai desert. What does their name mean? How did they use to live?

Camels have been used as transportation for a very long time. They were used by Ancient Egyptians as long ago as 3000 BCE. In North Africa today, millions of camels are still used every day for riding and for carrying goods across deserts.

Camels can grow to 1.85 meters and can run at speeds of 65 kilometers an hour. They also live a long time, 40–50 years. And they can cope[12] with the extreme temperatures in places like the Sahara Desert, where the days are boiling hot and the nights are freezing cold.

Camels are so good in the desert that even after trying wheeled vehicles like wagons and carriages, people actually went back to using them. Camels don't get stuck in the sand so easily!

[12]**cope:** find a way to live with problems or difficulties

Sometimes people who live in places with motor vehicles still prefer traditional transportation. The Amish are very traditional people who live quietly in separate communities in many parts of the world. They have strong religious beliefs that stop them from using engines or power machines. Instead, they travel in four-wheeled, horse-powered vehicles known as buggies.

Most Amish buggies now have a reflector on the back for safety.

The Amish have different types of buggies for different jobs. One type is the open two-seater for young couples to ride in. Families normally have a bigger buggy with a closed carriage to protect them from the weather. The market buggy is a wide, flat wagon for carrying goods to market.

There is, however, one change that has been made to these very traditional vehicles. After several accidents, most Amish now put reflectors on their buggies so they can be seen more easily at night.

Golf carts can carry people and their golf clubs.

CHAPTER 4

Unusual Transportation

LET'S TAKE A LOOK AT SOME OF THE MORE UNUSUAL WAYS TO GET FROM POINT A TO POINT B.

Sometimes, a car is just too big, but a bicycle might not carry all the things you need. For example, golfers have heavy clubs, and some golf courses are very large – several kilometers from start to finish. Carrying a bag of clubs for long distances isn't possible for some people, especially older people. But they want the fun and exercise of playing the game.

Enter the golf cart!

Golf carts are small, battery-powered cars that can carry both passengers and golf clubs. They are only designed to travel short distances at speeds of about 15 kilometers per hour. They may be slow, but so are the people in them! Golf carts are now popular as regular transportation in retirement communities – places where many older people live together.

?

ANALYZE

Why are different forms of transportation used in different situations?

Nowadays some people are choosing another new type of personal transportation: the Segway PT. This is a two-wheeled, battery-powered platform that is controlled by the rider's own weight.

When the rider moves forward, the Segway also moves forward. When the rider moves back, the Segway slows down. By leaning to the left or right, the rider can turn the vehicle in that direction.

Segways are capable of traveling as far as 38 kilometers on one battery charge and can reach speeds of about 20 kilometers per hour.

Although Segway PTs are not common, they are becoming more popular in crowded places. Tour groups find them a fun way to see the sights of a new city. Segways are not just expensive toys, however. Many are now also used for more serious jobs such as airport security and police patrols.

Security people use Segways in crowded areas.

ATVs are useful for off-road travel, and they're fun to drive, too.

Although some Segways have been designed with bigger wheels for traveling off-road, there are some environments that they just cannot handle. Many people living in the countryside or on farms use a much tougher form of transportation: the ATV, or All-Terrain Vehicle.

ATVs are like motorbikes, but with four wheels instead of two. The extra wheels allow them to handle much rougher terrain. For example, ATVs are often used by farmers to take food to animals in hard-to-reach places.

They are also used for fun. Some people race ATVs, and there are even competitions.

Video Quest

Hovercraft to the Rescue!

Watch this video about hovercrafts in Alaska. What are the main problems on the journey?

ATVs have trouble with one thing, though – snow. ATVs are heavy, so their big wheels just sink into deep snow. There is, however, a vehicle that has been specially designed to travel across snowy ground: the snowmobile.

At first sight, the snowmobile looks very similar to an ATV. It has handlebars and a motorbike-shaped body, and the rider's position is similar. But there is one big difference. Instead of wheels, the snowmobile has caterpillar tracks.

These wide, flat tracks stop the vehicle from sinking into the snow and move it along. At the front there is a ski that turns the vehicle left or right.

Snowmobiles have caterpillar tracks instead of wheels.

In areas of heavy snow, snowmobiles are people's cars and taxis. They are used to go to work, by scientists working in wildlife parks, and very importantly, by emergency services like search-and-rescue teams.

CHAPTER 5

What Do You Think?

HOW DO YOU NORMALLY GET AROUND? DO YOU WALK, GO BY CAR, OR TAKE SOME FORM OF PUBLIC TRANSPORTATION?

These days we all have to use some kind of transportation in our daily lives. We have to travel to school or work; or maybe we want to visit friends, go shopping, or go to a baseball game.

Look at the list of forms of transportation below. How suitable is each one to the place you live? Why? Would you consider using a form of transportation that you haven't used before?

Bicycle	Horse	Skateboard
Bus	Taxi	Motorcycle
Segway	Subway	Rickshaw

Think about the public transportation system in your area. How could it be improved?

Imagine that you have to plan a new public transportation system for your area. What would you do? What types of public transportation would you choose?

Here are some questions to think about:

- How much will it cost to set up the system?
- How will you get the money to pay for it?
- What building work will need to be done?
- What will be the effects on the environment?
- How will you get people to use the public transportation you provide?
- How will your system make your area safer?
- How do your ideas solve some of the present problems with transportation where you live?

Do you think you will see a system similar to yours in the future?

After You Read

Read the sentences and choose Ⓐ, Ⓑ, Ⓒ, or Ⓓ.

1 What is thought to be the earliest form of transportation?
- Ⓐ small boats
- Ⓑ wagons
- Ⓒ camels
- Ⓓ horses

2 What caused a big change in transportation in the 19th century?
- Ⓐ a network of roads
- Ⓑ the metal wheel
- Ⓒ a new kind of train
- Ⓓ a fast boat

3 Why did the popularity of public transportation decrease in the 20th century?
- Ⓐ Public transportation was more expensive.
- Ⓑ Public transportation was overcrowded.
- Ⓒ Private vehicles became less expensive to buy.
- Ⓓ Private vehicles became cheaper to use than buses.

4 How is Guangzhou trying to reduce pollution?
- Ⓐ By cutting the number of new cars on the road by half
- Ⓑ By encouraging bike use with new bicycle lanes
- Ⓒ By stopping people from using cars
- Ⓓ By stopping car production

5 Why did people start to use bicycles to power rickshaws?
- Ⓐ To be more environmentally friendly
- Ⓑ To reduce fuel costs
- Ⓒ Because they made the driver's work easier
- Ⓓ Because animals were banned

6 Why do camels make a good form of transportation in North Africa?

Ⓐ They don't cost very much.

Ⓑ They live a long time.

Ⓒ They know the desert routes well.

Ⓓ They cope well in extreme temperatures.

7 How are Segways driven?

Ⓐ By lifting your feet

Ⓑ By moving your body

Ⓒ Like motorbikes

Ⓓ Like golf carts

8 Where are ATVs used?

Ⓐ on golf courses

Ⓑ in the snow

Ⓒ in motorbike races

Ⓓ on rough terrain

True or False?

Read the sentences and decide if they are true (T) or false (F).

1 _____ Animals helped the growth of trade.

2 _____ The first wheels were probably made of stone.

3 _____ Bicycle lanes were built because they are cheap.

4 _____ Litters were used by rich and powerful people.

5 _____ Taxis in Venice have very small wheels.

6 _____ Elephants are used in Thailand for environmental reasons.

7 _____ The Amish make changes to their vehicles for safety reasons.

8 _____ ATVs have two wheels.

Answer Key

Words to Know, page 4
1 steam-powered **2** goods **3** vehicle **4** gasoline
5 congestion

Words to Know, page 5
1 ferry **2** Commuters **3** Transportation **4** bicycle lane
5 wagon **6** carriage

Predict, page 5
Answers will vary.

Video Quest, page 13
There are 50,000 taxis, 8 million train travelers, and
10 million plane travelers.

Understand, page 15
They are mainly used by tourists to see the sights.

Video Quest, page 18
Inhabitants/people of the desert. Following their herds of
animals in the desert.

Analyze, page 21
Answers will vary.

Video Quest, page 23
They have to be careful not to hit other vehicles or pieces
of ice during bad weather conditions. The vehicle is hard to
control.

Choose the Correct Answers, page 26
1 A **2** C **3** C **4** A **5** C **6** D **7** B **8** D

True or False?, page 27
1 T **2** F **3** F **4** T **5** F **6** F **7** T **8** F